ECOSYSTEMS
Ecology & The Environment

• • • • • • • • • • • • • • • • •

Written by Angela Wagner

GRADES 5 - 8
Reading Levels 3 - 4

Classroom Complete Press

P.O. Box 19729
San Diego, CA 92159
Tel: 1-800-663-3609 | Fax: 1-800-663-3608
Email: service@classroomcompletepress.com

www.classroomcompletepress.com

ISBN-13: 978-1-55319-366-1
ISBN-10: 1-55319-366-0

© **2007**

Critical Thinking Skills

Ecosystems

Skills For Critical Thinking	Reading Comprehension								Hands-On Activities
	Section 1	Section 2	Section 3	Section 4	Section 5	Section 6	Section 7	Section 8	
LEVEL 1 Knowledge									
• List Details/Facts	✓	✓	✓	✓	✓	✓	✓	✓	✓
• Recall Information	✓	✓	✓	✓	✓	✓	✓	✓	
• Match Vocab to Definitions	✓	✓		✓	✓	✓	✓		
• Define Vocabulary	✓		✓	✓			✓	✓	
• Label Diagrams				✓			✓		
• Recognize Validity (T/F)	✓	✓	✓		✓	✓			
LEVEL 2 Comprehension									
• Demonstrate Understanding	✓		✓	✓		✓	✓	✓	✓
• Explain Scientific Causation		✓	✓			✓			
• Rephrasing Vocab Meaning		✓	✓	✓			✓		
• Describe	✓				✓		✓		✓
• Classify into Scientific Groups					✓				
LEVEL 3 Application									
• Application to Own Life	✓		✓			✓	✓	✓	✓
• Model Scientific Process					✓			✓	
• Organize & Classify Facts	✓			✓				✓	
• Utilize Alternative Research Tools	✓	✓			✓		✓	✓	
LEVEL 4 Analysis									
• Distinguish Roles/Meanings		✓			✓				
• Make Inferences	✓		✓		✓	✓			✓
• Draw Conclusions Based on Facts Provided	✓		✓		✓		✓	✓	✓
• Classify Based on Facts Researched		✓	✓			✓			
LEVEL 5 Synthesis									
• Compile Research Information	✓	✓		✓	✓		✓		
• Design & Application	✓		✓	✓		✓			
• Create & Construct	✓		✓			✓	✓	✓	✓
• Imagine Self in Scientific Role		✓		✓		✓	✓		
LEVEL 6 Evaluation									
• State & Defend an Opinion		✓		✓		✓	✓		
• Justify Choices for Research Topics	✓	✓	✓	✓	✓		✓		
• Defend Selections & Reasoning			✓						✓

Based on Bloom's Taxonomy

Contents

🍎 TEACHER GUIDE

✏️ STUDENT HANDOUTS

EZ✓ EASY MARKING™ ANSWER KEY

✔ **6 BONUS** Activity Pages! **Additional worksheets for your students**
✔ **6 BONUS** Overhead Transparencies! **For use with your projection system**

FREE!

- Go to our website: **www.classroomcompletepress.com/bonus**
- Enter item CC4500 or Ecosystems
- Enter pass code CC4500D for Activity Pages. CC4500A for Overheads.

Assessment Rubric

• • • • • • • • • • • • • • • • • • • •

Ecosystems

Student's Name: _____ Assignment: _____ Level: _____

	Level 1	Level 2	Level 3	Level 4
Understanding Concepts	Demonstrates a limited understanding of concepts. Needs teacher intervention.	Demonstrates a basic understanding of concepts. Requires little teacher intervention.	Demonstrates a good understanding of concepts. Requires no teacher intervention.	Demonstrates a thorough understanding of concepts. Requires no teacher intervention.
Analysis and Application of Key Concepts	Limited application and interpretation in activity responses	Basic application and interpretation in activity responses	Good application and interpretation in activity responses	Strong application and interpretation in activity responses
Creativity and Imagination	Limited creativity and imagination applied in projects and activities	Some creativity and imagination applied in projects and activities	Satisfactory level of creativity and imagination applied in projects and activities	Beyond expected creativity and imagination applied in projects & activities
Application of Own Interests	Limited application of own interests in independent or group environment	Basic application of own interests in independent or group environment	Good application of own interests in independent or group environment	Strong application of own interests in independent or group environment

STRENGTHS:

WEAKNESSES:

NEXT STEPS:

Teacher Guide

Our resource has been created for ease of use by both TEACHERS and STUDENTS alike.

Introduction

This resource provides ready-to-use information and activities for remedial students in grades five to eight. Written to grade and using simplified language and vocabulary, science concepts are presented in a way that makes them more accessible to students and easier to understand. Comprised of reading passages, student activities and overhead transparencies, our resource can be used effectively for whole-class, small group and independent work.

How Is Our Resource Organized?

STUDENT HANDOUTS

Reading Passages and Activities (*in the form of reproducible worksheets*) make up the majority of our resource. The reading passages present important grade-appropriate information and concepts related to the topic. Embedded in each passage are one or more questions that ensure students understand what they have read.

For each reading passage there are BEFORE YOU READ activities and AFTER YOU READ activities.

- **The BEFORE YOU READ activities prepare students for reading by setting a purpose for reading. They stimulate background knowledge and experience, and guide students to make connections between what they know and what they will learn. Important concepts and vocabulary are also presented.**

- **The AFTER YOU READ activities check students' comprehension of the concepts presented in the reading passage and extend their learning. Students are asked to give thoughtful consideration of the reading passage through creative and evaluative short-answer questions, research, and extension activities.**

Hands-on Activities are included to further develop students' thinking skills and understanding of the concepts. The **Assessment Rubric** (*page 4*) is a useful tool for evaluating students' responses to many of the activities in our resource. The **Comprehension Quiz** (*page 48*) can be used for either a follow-up review or assessment at the completion of the unit.

PICTURE CUES

This resource contains three main types of pages, each with a different purpose and use. A **Picture Cue** at the top of each page shows, at a glance, what the page is for.

 Teacher Guide
- Information and tools for the teacher

 Student Handout
- Reproducible worksheets and activities

 Easy Marking™ Answer Key
- Answers for student activities

EASY MARKING™ ANSWER KEY

Marking students' worksheets is fast and easy with this **Answer Key**. Answers are listed in columns – just line up the column with its corresponding worksheet, as shown, and see how every question matches up with its answer!

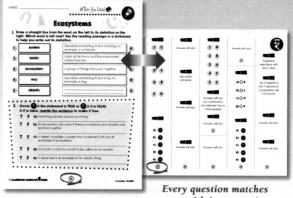

Every question matches up with its answer!

Bloom's Taxonomy

Our resource is an effective tool for any SCIENCE PROGRAM.

Bloom's Taxonomy* for Reading Comprehension

The activities in our resource engage and build the full range of thinking skills that are essential for students' reading comprehension and understanding of important science concepts. Based on the six levels of thinking in Bloom's Taxonomy, and using language at a remedial level, information and questions are given that challenge students to not only recall what they have read, but move beyond this to understand the text and concepts through higher-order thinking. By using higher-order skills of application, analysis, synthesis and evaluation, students become active readers, drawing more meaning from the text, attaining a greater understanding of concepts, and applying and extending their learning in more sophisticated ways.

Our resource, therefore, is an effective tool for any Science program. Whether it is used in whole or in part, or adapted to meet individual student needs, our resource provides teachers with essential information and questions to ask, inspiring students' interest, creativity, and promoting meaningful learning.

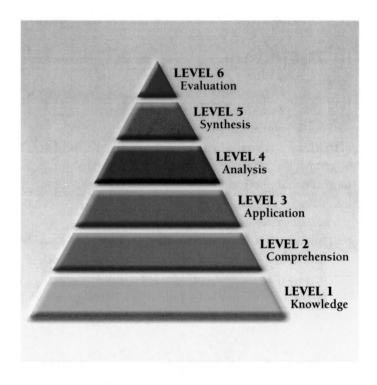

BLOOM'S TAXONOMY: 6 LEVELS OF THINKING

*Bloom's Taxonomy is a widely used tool by educators for classifying learning objectives, and is based on the work of Benjamin Bloom.

Vocabulary

- ecosystem • biotic • abiotic • system • environment • balance • organism • reproduce
- population • interbreed • succession • composition • producer • consumer • decomposer
- recycle • food web • food chain • interaction • nutrients • sugar • oxygen • photosynthesis
- carbon dioxide • leaves • energy • water cycle • evaporation • collection • precipitation
- condensation • microscope • virus • bacteria • microorganism • fungi

NAME: _____

Ecosystems

1. **Fill in the blanks using a word from the list below. You may use a dictionary to help.**

system	environment	balance	ecosystem	biotic	abiotic

a) The word _____ describes a group of things that work and live together in an environment.

b) Something that is living is described as being _____ .

c) A _____ is when all parts of a system work and live happily together.

d) A group of things that work together is called a _____ .

e) When something is not living, for example a rock, it is called _____ .

f) The whole area surrounding someone or something is called their _____ .

2. **List FIVE things that live in each of these places:**

Rainforest	Puddle	Handful of Soil	Planet Earth
_____	_____	_____	_____
_____	_____	_____	_____
_____	_____	_____	_____
_____	_____	_____	_____
_____	_____	_____	_____

3. Imagine you are stranded in the middle of a desert. Describe two living things and two non-living things that you might find there.

_____

_____

Ecosystems

What Is an Ecosystem?

Can you find two words in the bigger word, **"ECOSYSTEM"**? "Eco" means life forms and the environment in which they live. A "system" is a group of things that work together. Now put the two words back together.

An **ecosystem** is a group of things that work and live together in an environment. An example of an ecosystem is a rainforest, a pond, a city or even our Earth!

What Is an Ecosystem Made Of?

Everything we see can be put into two groups. If you look around, you will see both **biotic** and **abiotic** things. **Biotic** describes something that is living or was once alive. **Biotic** things include frogs, leaves, dead trees and humans. **Abiotic** means everything else that is not living. **Abiotic** things include rocks, cars, computers, and gold.

> **Describe your own example of an ecosystem. What BIOTIC and ABIOTIC things would you find in your ecosystem?**
>
> _____
>
> _____

How Big is an Ecosystem?

Ecosystems can be as big as a planet. They can also be as small as a puddle! Plants and animals live in ecosystems. Things that are too small to see also live in ecosystems. Everywhere you look, you can find an ecosystem.

Even a handful of soil is an ecosystem. There are many things living in soil. You may think that soil is just dirt. If you looked closely, you would find worms, bugs, sand and many more things. They are all part of the soil's ecosystem.

All parts of an ecosystem work and live together. They are just like people who live in the same neighborhood or city. Humans have jobs and so do things in an ecosystem. They need to work together to live and be happy. This makes the ecosystem balanced. Without a balance, the ecosystem will not work!

Ecosystems

1. **Draw a straight line from the word on the left to its definition on the right. Which word is left over? Use the reading passage or a dictionary to help you write out its definition.**

1	system	
2	biotic	
3	ecosystem	
4	eco	
5	abiotic	

A Describes something that is not living, for example, a computer

B Looks at life forms and the environment where they live

C A group of things that work together

D Describes something that is living, for example, a frog

E _____
_____

2. **Circle the word True if the statement is true. Circle the word False if it is false. If it is false, _rewrite the sentence_ to make it true.**

T   F   a) Everything we see around us is living.

_____

T   F   b) An ecosystem only works if there is a balance and all parts work and live together.

_____

T   F   c) A desert, a puddle, a jungle and our planet Earth are all examples of ecosystems.

_____

T   F   d) A handful of soil is too small to be called an ecosystem.

_____

T   F   e) A dead tree is an example of an abiotic thing.

_____

NAME: _____

Ecosystems

3. In what ways could your classroom be described as an ecosystem? Name two **abiotic** and two **biotic** things in your classroom.

_____

_____

4. Are all **ecosystems** the same size? Use examples to explain your answer.

_____

_____

Extension & Application

5. **Imagine you are a frog living somewhere in the world.** Use both your imagination and research tools to come up with facts about the ecosystem in which you live.

Copy the chart below onto a separate piece of paper to help you organize your thoughts and facts.

	Imagination	Research Tools
Where they live (i.e., water, soil)		
What they need to survive		
Biotic things found in their ecosystem		
Other abiotic things found in their ecosystem		

6. **TRAVEL TO AN ECOSYSTEM!** Design a **travel poster** which will convince people to come visit this ecosystem. Choose any ecosystem (try to think of one not yet mentioned) and use pictures and words to describe what you would find in this ecosystem. Remember… an ecosystem doesn't have to be a big place, and it has both biotic and abiotic things in it!

In your poster, be sure to include:
- The name of your ecosystem (a title)
- A slogan or sentence convincing people to come visit
- Drawings of both living and non-living things
- Research facts about the different parts of the ecosystem

NAME: _____

Populations

1. Draw a straight line from the word on the left to its definition on the right. You may use a dictionary to help.

1	organism	
2	reproduce	
3	population	
4	interbreed	
5	ecosystem	

A A group of similar individuals living in the same geographic area

B To produce offspring or children which increases a population

C A group of things that live and work together in the same environment

D A living thing such as a plant or animal

E To reproduce with another organism within the same population

2. Use a dictionary to look up the word INTERACTION. Write the definition below.

The dictionary definition of an **interaction** is:

_____

_____

3. Think about the last **interaction** you had with someone before you started this activity. Describe who the interaction was between. Then come up with your own definition of an **interaction**.

_____

_____

_____

_____

  NAME: _____

Populations

Let us go back and remind ourselves what an **ecosystem** is. We can remember that it is made up of small groups of things that interact with each other. They interact with each other in an environment. What do we mean by these "things'? These interacting things are called organisms. An **organism** is any individual form of life. An example of an organism is a plant or an animal.

An organism cannot live or interact by itself. It needs another organism in its ecosystem to interact with. Since many organisms live in an ecosystem, there will be many organisms that are similar. We call this group of similar organisms a population. A **population** is a group of similar individuals living in the same geographic area. For example, a field full of sunflowers next to a field where there are no sunflowers is a population. An area of water that contains many killer whales is also an example of a population.

Can you think of another example of a population?

_____

_____

_____

It is important to remember two things about populations. First, these individual organisms need to be similar. To be similar, they need to look similar, eat similar food, move in a similar way, and so on. Second, they need to live in the same area. A killer whale that lives in one ocean is not part of the same population as a killer whale that lives in another ocean.

Populations

For example, there are many killer whales that live on our planet. A killer whale population would only include whales that live together and interbreed. If they do not, they are not part of the same population.

How Do Populations Grow?

All populations change over time. Populations may grow or they may shrink. We know that human populations grow. So do populations of things other than humans. They grow because organisms in the same population **interbreed**. This means that organisms only **reproduce** with other organisms in the same population. When organisms **reproduce**, the number of organisms in a population increases.

Explain why the population in the city you live in might get bigger or smaller.

_____

_____

It can be difficult for a population to survive in an ecosystem. A population has a certain number of organisms in it. This number needs to stay the same to survive. This number goes up if organisms reproduce. This number can also go down. The number goes down if organisms do not reproduce. If they do not reproduce, the population will not survive.

Populations

1. Put a check mark (✓) next to the answer that best finishes the sentence.

a) An ecosystem is made up of a small group of things that...
- ○ **A**   have never seen each other before.
- ○ **B**   interact with each other.
- ○ **C**   all live in different parts of the world.
- ○ **D**   all look exactly the same.

b) An organism is...
- ○ **A**   anything that is so small you can not see it with your own eyes.
- ○ **B**   an animal that has all the organs that humans have.
- ○ **C**   any individual form of life.
- ○ **D**   a group of things that live and work together in a small environment.

c) A population is a group of similar individuals that...
- ○ **A**   eat different kinds of food.
- ○ **B**   live in different locations but still look similar.
- ○ **C**   do not interact with other individuals in their population.
- ○ **D**   live in the same geographic area.

d) An example of a population is...
- ○ **A**   all the monkeys that live in Earth.
- ○ **B**   a group of Great White sharks that live in the Pacific Ocean.
- ○ **C**   a group of people that live in Florida and another group of people that live in Texas.
- ○ **D**   all colonies of ants that live in different sandy beaches.

2. Circle the word True if the statement is true. Circle the word False if it is false.

T   F   a) It is difficult to find many similar organisms in an ecosystem.

T   F   b) A population is a group of individuals that are similar but may live in different parts of the world.

T   F   c) A group of dolphins living in the Pacific Ocean is a good example of a population.

T   F   d) Populations do not grow because they do not reproduce.

T   F   e) If the number of organisms in a population goes down, the population can still survive.

Populations

Answer the questions in complete sentences.

3. How does a **population** grow?

_____

4. Can it be difficult for a **population** to survive in an **ecosystem**? Explain why or why not.

_____

_____

Extension & Application

5. Copy and complete the chart below. Come up with an example of a population for the organism on the left side of the chart. Then come up with an example that would <u>not</u> be a good example of a population. The first question has been completed for you.

Organism	Population example	Not a population example
Monkey	All the curly-tailed monkeys that live in South Africa	
Maple tree		
Worm		
Snake		
Daisy flower		

6. CALLING ALL WRITERS AND ARTISTS!

Pick an organism from the list above and complete ONLY ONE of the following projects, either Project A or Project B. If you need help, you can use research tools to find information about your organism. Don't forget to use your imagination too!

Project A: STORY

Write a story about the organism you have chosen to be. Be sure to include the following: introduce who you are, who is part of your population, where you live, and any other information that describes what life is like to be your organism.

Project B: DRAWING

Draw a population picture! Use your imagination to draw a full-page picture showing you (the organism you have chosen) and your population. By looking at your picture you should be able to see: what organism you have chosen, who is part of your population, where you live, and any other details you think are important.

NAME: _____

Change in Ecosystems

1. **a)** What does the word **balance** mean to you?

_____

_____

b) Can you think of situations where balance is **very** important? One line has already been filled for you. Can you think of **four** more?

Balancing on a tightrope in a circus _____

1 _____

2 _____

3 _____

4 _____

2. Complete each sentence with a word from the list. You may use a dictionary to help.

population   succession   ecosystem   biotic   environment   composition

a) [_____] describes what happens when something changes over a long period of time.

b) The word that describes a group of things that work and live together in an environment is an [_____].

c) In an ecosystem, you will find abiotic things (non-living things) and [_____] things (living things).

d) The [_____] where someone or something lives includes the whole area surrounding them.

e) The [_____] of a jar of jellybeans includes all the different colors of jellybeans that are in the jar.

f) A group of similar individuals living in the same geographic area is called a [_____].

Change in Ecosystems

Do Ecosystems Change Over Time?

Everything that lives in our world changes over time. Humans change. Our bodies change. Animals change. Plants change. Every living thing changes over time, including ecosystems. What an ecosystem looks like changes, and so does its composition. The **composition** of an ecosystem describes everything that is part of an ecosystem. This includes both living and non-living things, both biotic and abiotic things.

Look around you right now. Pick the first thing you see. Describe how it changes over time.

_____

_____

_____

_____

When an ecosystem changes over a long period of time, it is called **succession**. The populations in an ecosystem change during succession. A population may become smaller over time. A population may even disappear completely. A population may become much bigger. Something else may happen during succession. Species from ecosystems close by might come and move into the ecosystem. These are all changes that may happen to an ecosystem over time. They are all part of succession. An ecosystem might also change because of humans. For example, when we develop land for houses, we cut down trees. We change the environment for all plants and animals. Some animals can adapt to the change. Others can not. Their population is then affected.

NAME: _____

Change in Ecosystems

1. Write the answer that best completes the sentences below.

a) [_____] (**Some / Every**) living thing changes over time.

b) Animals and plants change over time. [_____] (**Ecosystems / Atmospheres**) also change over time.

c) The [_____] (**energy / composition**) of an ecosystem includes both biotic and abiotic things.

d) Populations in an ecosystem [_____] (**change / stay the same**) during succession.

e) An ecosystem might change because of natural causes but it may also change because of [_____] (**heavy rain / humans**).

2. Circle the word True if the statement is true. Circle the word False if it is false.

T   F   **a)** Humans, animals, and plants change over time but ecosystems do not change over time.

T   F   **b)** The composition of an ecosystem describes everything that is part of an ecosystem.

T   F   **c)** When an ecosystem changes over a long period of time, it is called evolution.

T   F   **d)** During succession, a population may get bigger but it might also disappear completely.

T   F   **e)** Cutting down trees, building houses, and dumping garbage are all examples of how humans can harmfully affect an ecosystem.

Change in Ecosystems

3. What is the composition of an ecosystem?

_____

_____

4. How can an ecosystem change over time during **succession**?

_____

_____

5. Describe how humans can have a large **impact** on an ecosystem. Give at least two examples.

_____

_____

Extension & Application

6. SAVE OUR ECOSYSTEMS T-shirt Design Contest!

You have already read about how humans can harm an ecosystem. Cutting down trees for houses is one way. Can you think of another one?

You have been entered into a T-shirt design contest. **Your task is to design a T-shirt that shows what humans can do to stop harming our ecosystems.** Pick ONE harmful human activity and use it for your T-shirt design.

Your T-shirt should have:
- a slogan (a sentence telling humans what to stop doing, for example, "Stop Cutting Down Trees!")
- words and pictures that support your slogan

Harmful human activity chosen: _____

Slogan on T-shirt: _____

Remember, be creative and design a T-shirt that you would like to wear!

T-Shirt Design Contest!

Write "Save Our Ecosystems!" on the line in the shirt

Producers, Consumers & Decomposers

1. **Produce, consume, decompose.** What do these words mean? Look up these three words. <u>First</u>, use a dictionary to write down the word's definition. <u>Second</u>, use the word in your own sentence, showing that you understand its meaning.

A **produce**

    Dictionary: _____

    Own sentence: _____

B **consume**

    Dictionary: _____

    Own sentence: _____

C **decompose**

    Dictionary: _____

    Own sentence: _____

2. **Complete each sentence with a word from the list. You may use a dictionary to help.**

| producers | sun | consumer | recycle | decomposer |

a) The [＿＿＿＿＿] is the main source of energy for everything on our Earth. It gives off light and heat.

b) [＿＿＿＿＿] are things that break down material in dead organisms.

c) We [＿＿＿＿＿] things so that we can use them again.

d) Something that can make its own food is called a [＿＿＿＿＿].

e) A [＿＿＿＿＿] is something that uses something else to get food and energy.

Producers, Consumers & Decomposers

All organisms in an ecosystem get energy from the same place. All energy comes from the Sun. Green plants absorb this energy. This energy is then shared with all parts of an ecosystem. Every organism in an ecosystem gets their energy and food a different way. This divides all organisms into three kinds: **producers**, **consumers**, and **decomposers**. The difference between these three kinds of organisms is the way they find food and energy. Let us now look at the three different kinds now.

STOP

Think about your favorite food. Explain how the Sun played an important role in its growth.

_____

_____

_____

A **producer** is an organism that produces its own food. An example of a producer is a green plant. It takes in energy from the Sun and makes food which is then passed on to **consumers**. A **consumer** is an organism that cannot make its own food. It is called a **consumer** because it depends on others. It gets food by eating other organisms. **Decomposers** play a very important role too. **Decomposers** break down materials in dead organisms. Humans recycle certain things so that we can use them again. **Decomposers** do the same thing. They recycle nutrients from dead organisms and return them to the soil. They can then be used again by **producers**. Imagine that these three kinds of organisms all live in a cycle. They all depend on each other for energy and food. Without each other, they would not survive.

Producers, Consumers & Decomposers

1. **Draw a line between two circles to match up the words with their definitions.**

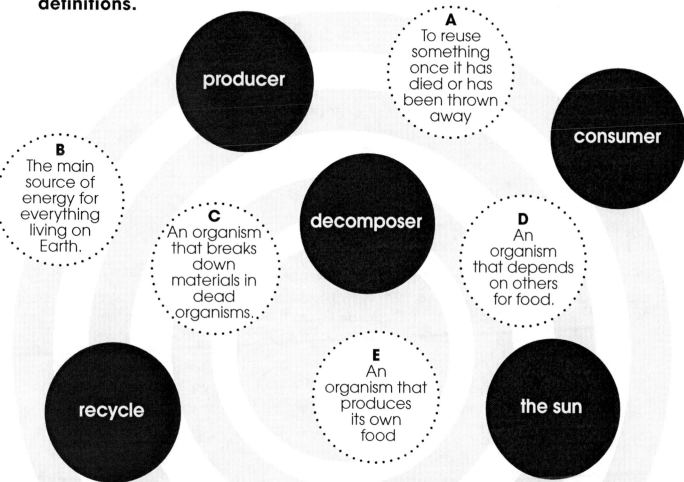

producer

A
To reuse something once it has died or has been thrown away

consumer

B
The main source of energy for everything living on Earth.

C
An organism that breaks down materials in dead organisms.

decomposer

D
An organism that depends on others for food.

recycle

E
An organism that produces its own food

the sun

Answer the questions in complete sentences.

2. In what way can we divide all organisms? Use words from the reading passage in your answer.

_____

_____

3. What is the difference between a **producer** and a **consumer**?

_____

_____

Producers, Consumers & Decomposers

~~~
**Answer the questions in complete sentences.**

**4.** What is the role of a **decomposer**?

_____

_____

**5.** How do producers, consumers, and decomposers all live in a **cycle**?

_____

_____
~~~

Extension & Application

6. **Imagine you have just bought your own business.** Right now you have too much work so you need to hire some people to work for you. You will need to hire a **PRODUCER**, a **CONSUMER**, and a **DECOMPOSER**. These jobs do not exist in the human world, but for this activity, use your imagination.

You have been given space to advertise these three jobs in the local newspaper. What would you write? Copy down the chart below onto your own piece of paper. You can come up with your own design or you can follow the format below.

You should have **THREE** advertisements to complete this activity, one for each job: **producer**, **consumer**, and **decomposer**.

Newspaper Name - Classifieds

Today's Date: _____

Looking for a: _____

Job Description: _____

_____

Salary: _____

Please Apply by: _____

NAME: _____

Food Chains & Food Webs

1. **In the square below, draw what you think a chain looks like. Fill the whole square!**

a) How does the chain stay together?

_____

_____

_____

_____

b) What would happen if you took out one of the chain links?

_____

_____

_____

2. **Complete each sentence with a word from the list. Use a dictionary to help you.**

organism	web	chain	interaction	nutrients

a) A [_____] is a complicated structure. Spiders spin them!

b) A relationship between two or more things is called an [_____].

c) [_____] are the healthy things found in food that helps things grow.

d) An [_____] is any individual form of life, for example, a plant or an animal.

e) A [_____] has links in it that are connected. These links hold the chain together.

NAME: _____

Food Chains & Food Webs

What Is a Food Chain?

We just learned that all organisms depend on each other for food and energy. We also learned that all food is produced using the Sun's energy. Some organisms use the Sun's energy directly for food (for example, plants). Others eat other organisms because they cannot make their own food. And others break down nutrients in dead organisms to make food for others. We call these producers, consumers, and decomposers. If you look at the drawing to the right, you will see many arrows. These arrows show how each organism is dependent on another organism. It looks like a long chain. We call this the **food chain**. Each part is linked or dependent on another part.

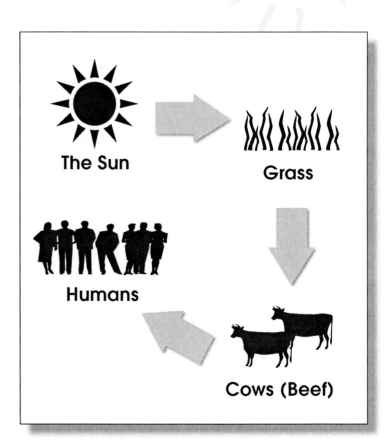

The Sun

Grass

Humans

Cows (Beef)

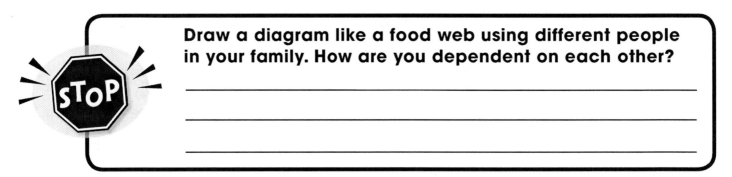

Draw a diagram like a food web using different people in your family. How are you dependent on each other?

_____

_____

_____

Do humans only eat one type of food? Of course not. There are no organisms that eat only one type of food. Every organism depends on more than one other organism for food. That is why the **food chain** looks very busy. In a food chain diagram, every organism would have more than one arrow coming towards it or going away from it. The arrows overlap each other. Have you ever looked closely at a spider's web? The many arrows in a food chain look very similar to a spider's web. That is why we call the busy interactions between organisms a **food web**.

Food Chains & Food Webs

1. Circle the word True if the statement is true. Circle the word False if it is false. If it is false, **rewrite the sentence** to make it true.

T   F   **a)** All organisms use the Sun's energy directly for food.

_____

T   F   **b)** Some organisms eat other organisms because they can not make their own food.

_____

T   F   **c)** Arrows in a food web diagram show how organisms depend on other organisms.

_____

T   F   **d)** Not all parts of a food chain are linked.

_____

T   F   **e)** Organisms depend on only one other organism for food.

_____

2. Draw a straight line from the word on the left to its definition on the right. Which word is left over? Use the reading passage or a dictionary to help you write out its definition.

1	nutrients		A relationship between two or more things	A
2	food chain		Healthy things found in food that helps things grow	B
3	organism		Any individual form of life	C
4	food web		A diagram showing many food chains. The many arrows show the busy interactions between organisms.	D
5	interaction		_____	E

Food Chains & Food Webs

3. **A food chain diagram** shows how organisms depend on each other for food. Look at the food chain diagram below. Explain in your own words how these organisms depend on each other.

The Sun

⬇

Grass

⬇

Cows (Beef)

⬇

Humans

_____

_____

_____

_____

_____

_____

Extension & Application

4. SPIN YOUR OWN FOOD WEB!

Food webs look like spider webs. They show how EACH organism depends on MANY organisms for food. Many arrows criss-cross over each other. This shows how complicated their interactions are.

On the worksheet provided, create your own **food web**. The first box is filled in for you (the Sun). Fill in the rest of the boxes using organisms from the list below. **CHOOSE EIGHT** from the list of twenty organisms. Use research tools to find out what each organism eats. Remember, each organism is dependent on more than one other organism! Use **arrows** to show how these organisms are dependent on each other.

- Humans
- Worm
- Rabbit
- Grass
- Chicken
- Cow
- Rice

- A Deer
- Seaweed
- Lettuce
- Wheat
- Beetle
- Dog
- Mouse

- Corn
- Ant
- Fish
- Carrot
- Potato
- Shark

NAME: _____

Spin Your Own Food Web!

Fill in the boxes using **organisms** from the list (page 28). Find out what each organism eats. Use arrows to show who each organism is dependent on for food. Remember, there should be many arrows. Each organism is dependent on more than one other organism!

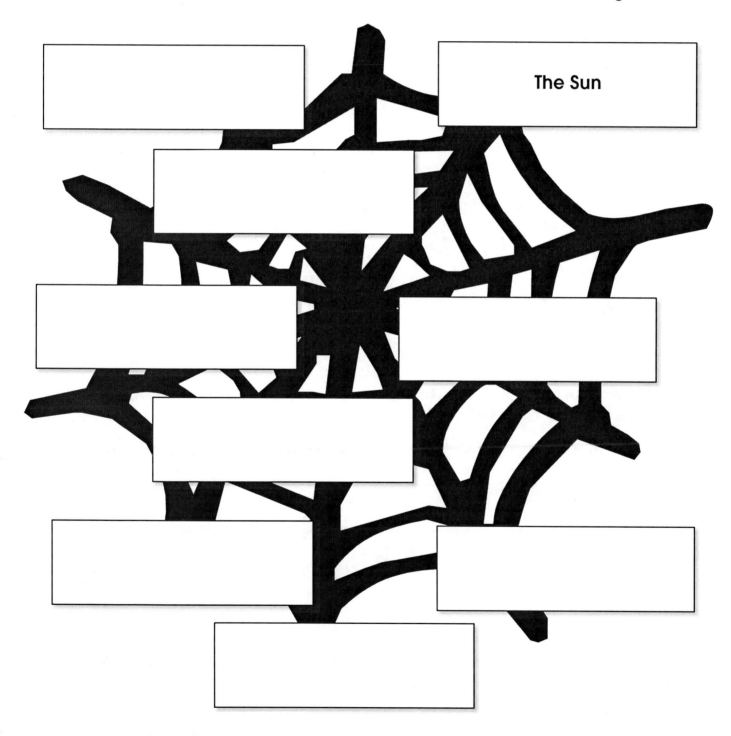

The Sun

Ecosystems CC4500

Photosynthesis

1. Complete each sentence with a word from the list below. You can use a dictionary for help.

> sugar   oxygen   photosynthesis   carbon dioxide   leaves   energy

a) The word _____ describes the way that green plants make their own food.

b) We need food to give us _____ so that we can live a healthy life.

c) Just like humans have arms and legs to collect food, plants have _____ to help them make their own food.

d) When humans breathe in fresh air, we breathe in oxygen and breathe out

_____ .

e) _____ is very sweet but is not only used by humans to sweeten food. Plants use it too to make food!

f) A gas that is produced by plants during photosynthesis is called _____ .

2. Read the words below. In which group does each thing belong – PLANTS or ANIMALS?

> cactus   monkey   small tree   human   rose bush   snake   puppy

PLANTS	ANIMALS

3. Pick TWO things from the above list. Where do you think they get energy from?

a) A _____ gets energy from _____ .

b) A _____ gets energy from _____ .

NAME: _____

Photosynthesis

Did you know that most plants are very lucky? Plants are lucky because they never need to go grocery shopping! They also do not need to spend time cooking! They sit around in soil and wait for sunshine to come. Plants use the Sun to make their food themselves. Humans make food by cooking. We cannot make our own food without buying it or growing it. Plants are the only living things that can make their own food.

Animals breathe in oxygen and breathe out **carbon dioxide**. Green plants do the opposite. They breathe in carbon dioxide and breathe out oxygen. Plants breathe in carbon dioxide through their leaves during the day. From sunlight, green plants mix carbon dioxide and water to make **sugar** and **oxygen**. We all like sugar, don't we? Plants do too. Sugar gives plants energy to grow. We call this whole process **photosynthesis**. It is the process where plants use sunlight, water and carbon dioxide to make food, oxygen and water.

Why do you think photosynthesis is the most important process on the Earth?

_____

_____

_____

Many animals and plants depend on other plants to survive. That is why **photosynthesis** is so important. If plants could not use the Sun's energy to make food, what would happen? We would not be able to live! Light is so important to plants and plants are so important to us. We can eat so many different things that plants can grow… fruits, nuts, leaves, seeds, and even flowers!

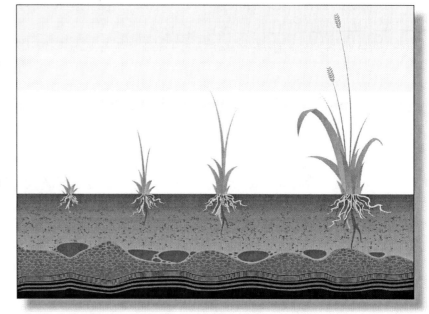

NAME: _____

Photosynthesis

1. Put a check mark (✓) next to the answer that is most correct.

a) We can consider plants to be very lucky because:

- ○ **A**   they have leaves to help them grow strong and tall.
- ○ **B**   they are the only living organisms that are able to make their own food.
- ○ **C**   their roots bring them food from the soil.
- ○ **D**   they grow very close to other plants and can help each other find food.

b) How do plants make their own food?

- ○ **A**   They find bugs and other things in the soil close to their roots.
- ○ **B**   They do not need food to grow.
- ○ **C**   They get food from the plants that are living close to them.
- ○ **D**   They use sunlight, water and carbon dioxide to make food.

c) Why is photosynthesis the most important process on our Earth?

- ○ **A**   Many animals and plants depend on plants to survive.
- ○ **B**   Plants do not need energy from sunlight to make food.
- ○ **C**   We would still survive on Earth if plants didn't make food.
- ○ **D**   Only humans depend on plants for energy.

d) Where do plants get most of their energy from?

- ○ **A**   From the people that have planted them in the soil.
- ○ **B**   From water, either from a garden hose or rain.
- ○ **C**   From the air around them, especially on hot summer days.
- ○ **D**   From the sun's energy which is called solar energy.

2. Circle the word True if the statement is true. Circle the word False if it is false. If it is false, <u>rewrite the sentence</u> to make it true.

T   F   a) We can eat everything that plants grow, even some flowers.

_____

T   F   b) Humans breathe in carbon dioxide and breathe out oxygen. Plants do the same.

_____

T   F   c) Humans can make their own food just like plants.

_____

Photosynthesis

3. Circle the words that plants use to help them make their own food:

water   vitamins   oxygen   carbon dioxide   Mars bar   sunlight

4. Circle the words that are a part of the photosynthesis process:

plants   humans   sunlight   fertilizer   energy   water

5. Circle the things that are able to make their own food:

chef   tree   child   cactus   worm   fern   plant

Extension & Application

6. Imagine You Are The Sun. You have a huge job on this Earth. Write a **DIARY ENTRY** or a **LETTER** to a friend telling them all about what your day is like as the Sun. Use your imagination as best as you can. Be sure to include specific information you have learned from the reading passage:

- Who is depending on you for energy?
- How does that help other things living on Earth?
- How does your energy help others make food?

Your diary entry should look similar to the following:

Today's Date (month, day, year): _____
Dear Diary (or friend's name),
_____
_____
Sincerely, (your name)

7. PRETEND YOU ARE A TEACHER! Using what you have learned from the reading passage, DESIGN A DIAGRAM which would help you explain the process of **photosynthesis** to another student. Remember: assume that the other student knows very little about plants and energy. Be sure to label your diagram!

You should include the following things in your diagram… Don't forget to use arrows to show relationships between two things!

the sun   water   oxygen   carbon dioxide   sugar   food

The Water Cycle

1. **Draw a straight line from the word on the left to its definition on the right. You may use a dictionary to help.**

1 water cycle	**A** Gathering of objects
2 evaporation	**B** The movement of water from land up into the air and then back to the ground
3 collection	**C** Water or the amount of water that falls to the Earth
4 precipitation	**D** Water turns into vapor or steam
5 condensation	**E** Water turns from a vapor into a liquid

2. **Complete each sentence with a word from the list below. You can use a dictionary for help.**

collection   water   evaporation   condensation   precipitation

a) _____ is when water falls down to the Earth as rain, snow or hail.

b) When you boil water in a tea kettle, steam is produced. This is called

_____ .

c) _____ can be a solid, liquid, or a gas.

d) _____ is when you are gathering something together in

one place.

e) When water turns from a vapor into a liquid, it is called _____ .

The Water Cycle

Pretend there is a full glass of water sitting on your desk right now. Look at the water. Guess how old the water is. Have you ever thought about that? You might have just turned on the tap a minute ago. Does that make the water one minute old? No, it does not. The water might have fallen from the sky a week ago. That still does not make the water one week old. The water itself has been around pretty much as long as the Earth has. It is <u>very</u> old! Think way back to when life on Earth started. The water in your glass was part of the very first ocean. The Earth has an exact amount of water on it. When water goes around and around on our Earth, we call it the **water cycle**.

Where do you think tap water comes from? Where do you think it goes once it goes down the drain?

_____

_____

_____

_____

The water cycle is made up of four steps: evaporation, condensation, precipitation, and collection. **Evaporation** is the first step. The Sun heats up the water in lakes and oceans. The water turns into vapor or steam. **Condensation** is the next step. Water vapor in the air gets cold and turns back into a liquid. Clouds are formed! **Precipitation** happens when so much water has condensed that air cannot hold it anymore. Clouds let water fall back to Earth. This is rain and snow! **Collection** happens when precipitation falls back to Earth. Water goes into lakes and oceans. It may also fall onto land and soak into the Earth through the soil. Then the cycle starts all over again!

NAME: _____

The Water Cycle

1. **Number the events from ① to ④ in the order they occur in the WATER CYCLE.**

_____ **a) Condensation:** Water vapor in the air gets cold and turns back into a liquid. Clouds are formed.

_____ **b) Precipitation:** So much water has condensed that air can not hold it anymore.

_____ **c) Collection:** Precipitation falls back to Earth through lakes, oceans and through the soil in land.

_____ **d) Evaporation:** The Sun heats up from lakes, oceans and land. Water is turned into vapor or steam.

2. **Label the diagram below using words from the list.**

| precipitation | condensation | evaporation | collection |

B: _____

A: _____

C: _____

D: _____

The Water Cycle

3. **Circle** the word True if the statement is true. **Circle** the word False if it is false. If it is false, <u>rewrite the sentence</u> to make it true.

T   F   a) Tap water might have fallen from the sky as rain water.

_____

T   F   b) Water from the tap has just been created on Earth.

_____

T   F   c) The amount of water on Earth changes every day.

_____

T   F   d) Evaporation is the last step in the water cycle. It is when water falls back to Earth as rain or snow.

_____

T   F   e) The water cycle shows how water goes around and around on Earth.

_____

Extension & Application

4. **WRITE A PLAY!**

You are the newest play writer in Hollywood. You have a very important job to do. Five hundred people are coming to watch your play called "The Water Cycle" but you haven't written it yet!

You will write a play that will teach the audience how **water cycles around on Earth.** Create a CONVERSATION between the following characters/actors:

- Water
- Evaporation
- Condensation
- Precipitation
- Collection

Use your conversation to explain what happens to the "water" character at each of these stages in the water cycle. Pretend each stage is a character!

Be creative and use your own sense of humor. A funny play is an enjoyable play!

Microorganisms

1. **A microscope** is used to see something that is too small to see with your own eyes. Pick **THREE** things from the list below. **Draw** what you think they would look like under a microscope. Remember, your drawing will be very close up to the object!

> Leaf   Worm   Fingerprint   Corn   Spider   Grass   Grain of rice

[drawing box]   [drawing box]   [drawing box]

_____   _____   _____

2. **Fill in the blanks using a word from the list below. You may use a dictionary to help.**

> virus   microscope   bacteria   microorganism   fungi

a) A [_____] is used to look at something that is too small to see with your own eyes.

b) An organism that needs to be magnified to be seen is called a [_____].

c) [_____] are microorganisms that have only one cell.

d) If someone gets sick with a cold, they have caught a [_____].

e) Organisms that live by taking in nutrients from organic things are called [_____].

Microorganisms

What Is a Microorganism?

Imagine something that is so small that you can not see it with your own eyes. Have you ever used a **microscope** in science class to look at something very, very small? Well, you would need to use a microscope if you wanted to look at a microorganism. A **microorganism** is any organism that needs to be magnified to be seen.

Microorganisms are incredibly small but are very important on our Earth. They have a job to do. They are so important that without them, life on Earth would not exist. They recycle dead matter so that it can be reused in the environment.

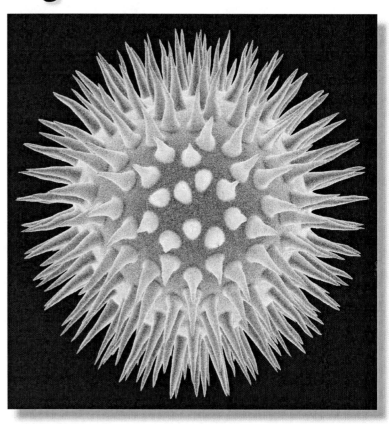

STOP

How do you think bread gets so fluffy and full of air?

_____

_____

_____

Microorganisms include small organisms such as **bacteria, fungi**, and **viruses**. Many microorganisms are useful and some are harmful. Fortunately, most microorganisms are harmless. Humans use microorganisms in our lives every day, but we might not even realize it. For example, fungi are used by doctors to help people feel better. They are also used in making some foods, like cheese and yogurt. Some microorganisms are harmful though. They can cause infections. An infection is caused by a harmful microorganism that is passed from one person to another. Have you ever had a cold because someone else in your class had a cold too? You can see that bacteria can be passed on very easily. It is important to take care of yourself so that you avoid these harmful microorganisms!

NAME: _____

Microorganisms

1. Put a check mark (✔) next to the answer that is most correct.

a) What could you use to look at something so small you couldn't see it with your eyes?
- ○ **A** A microphone.
- ○ **B** A microscope.
- ○ **C** A telescope.
- ○ **D** A new prescription for your glasses.

b) What very important job do microorganisms do on Earth?
- ○ **A** They reproduce with other organisms in their population.
- ○ **B** They organize the lives of organisms in their ecosystem.
- ○ **C** They recycle dead matter so that it can be reused in the environment.
- ○ **D** They don't actually have an important job to do.

c) Microorganisms include which of the following?
- ○ **A** Sunlight, oxygen and carbon dioxide.
- ○ **B** Bacteria, food and energy.
- ○ **C** Producers, consumers and decomposers.
- ○ **D** Bacteria, yeasts, fungi and viruses.

d) How do we use microorganisms in a helpful way?
- ○ **A** To help us learn about the environment we live in.
- ○ **B** To pass infections from one person to another.
- ○ **C** To make some foods and medicine.
- ○ **D** To teach us how to recycle things rather than throwing them in the garbage.

e) How early can microorganisms be passed on from person to person?
- ○ **A** Microorganisms can never be passed on from person to person.
- ○ **B** Microorganisms can be passed on very easily, just like with the common cold.
- ○ **C** People don't have to avoid harmful microorganisms so bacteria does not matter.
- ○ **D** All microorganisms are harmless so it is good when they get passed on from person to person.

Microorganisms

2. **Divide the word MICROORGANISM into two parts: MICRO and ORGANISM.** Use a dictionary to look up the definitions of both words. Then put both parts back together and write your own definition of microorganism.

A **Micro** (dictionary): _____

B **Organism** (dictionary): _____

C Own definition of **microorganism**:

_____

Extension & Application

3. **Be a Virus Detective!**

Send out a warning statement. Choose ONE virus from the list below. Use an encyclopedia, a dictionary and the internet to research the virus. Use the format below to begin your "Warning" statement. In your warning, you should include:

- The virus name
- How the virus is harmful
- How it is passed from one person to another

Influenza	measles	Norwalk	herpes	HIV

WARNING: Virus Found	
Virus name:	
Information:	

4. **The Secret Ingredient to Bread!**

For this activity, pretend you are a baker. You will **RESEARCH A RECIPE** to make bread. Use the chart below to fill in a recipe card. Make sure you use step-by-step instructions. Don't forget to include yeast. It's the secret ingredient!

Recipe _____

Ingedients:

Step 1: _____

Step 2: _____

Step 3: _____

The Rabbit Bean Population!

YOU WILL NEED:

• Two colors of dried beans
• Graph paper
• Pencil or marker

Begin with two beans. You should have two different colored beans. One bean is a **male** rabbit and the other color bean is a **female** rabbit.

You are now going to **record the rabbit population for the next five years**. You won't be spending five real years on this project, don't worry!

Each year, each pair of rabbits gives birth to two rabbits – one male and one female. **SET UP A GRAPH** to record how the rabbit population will grow. Each year you will add beans to your population pile. These beans will be the new rabbits that are born each year. Record the numbers on your graph paper.

How many rabbits are in the population after five years? **Remember: after the first year, there are many pairs that will give birth to two new rabbits. The population will grow quickly!**

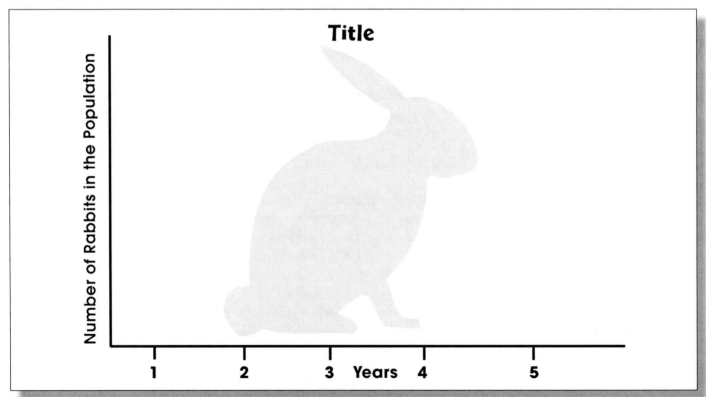

Title

Number of Rabbits in the Population

1   2   3   Years   4   5

A Scientist Investigates an Ecosystem!

FOR THIS ACTIVITY, you will need to gather or find the following things:

An outdoor area (for example, the school field or a patch of a garden)
- **A long piece of string**
- **Magnifying glass**
- **Thermometer**
- **Popsicle sticks**
- **Paper and pencil**
- **Small gardening tools**

WHAT YOU WILL DO:

1. Pick a small patch of land to investigate.
2. Use the string to mark off the area you have chosen.
3. On your piece of paper, record everything you can see about your ecosystem. Include all biotic (living) and abiotic (non-living) things. How are these organisms working and living together?
4. Using the thermometer, record temperatures in your ecosystem.
5. Turn over a small patch of grass or flip over a rock. Record what you see beneath the surface.

Now it's time to record your conclusions!

IN YOUR RECORDS, answer the following questions:

- Consider the variety of biotic and abiotic things you found in your ecosystem. Which was the largest population?

  _____

- How do each of these organisms survive in your ecosystem?

  _____

- Can you think of any other populations that could survive in your ecosystem?

  _____

- Can you think of any populations which would <u>not</u> survive in your ecosystem? Why not?

  _____

Hands-On Activity #3

Build Your Own Ecosystem!

**We have talked and read about so many ecosystems.
Now it is time to build your own!**

COLLECT THE FOLLOWING MATERIALS:

- Gravel or small rocks
- Soil/dirt
- A jar or bottle (with a large enough top to put your hand into)
- A lid for your jar or bottle to seal it
  (you can seal it with tape if you think air can get into the jar)
- A few plants from the school yard or a garden
- Small animals from the garden
  (worms, snails, slugs, etc.)
- Wood, garden rocks or branches to make it look
  like a real ecosystem

WHAT YOU WILL DO:

1. Put a large handful of gravel or small rocks in the bottom of your jar.
2. Add a large handful of soil.
3. Plant the plants into the soil. Try to choose plants that fit into your jar. If it's a small jar, only use small plants. If you put too many plants in, they will not survive!
4. If you think your ecosystem needs water, add a bit of water. Don't over water your ecosystem though!
5. **This is the fun bit...** choose some animals. Use anything you can find in the school yard or garden. Remember, choose small animals. You want these animals to survive!
6. Close your ecosystem. Put the lid on or use tape to seal it.

Now it's time to record your observations!

ON A PIECE OF PAPER, record the following things:

- Size of your container (you may want to draw a picture of your ecosystem)
- Number and type of plants and animals you used
- How much soil you used
- What is happening in your system? Count your animals and record if your plants are growing. Have all of your plants and animals survived?

Have fun building your own ecosystem!

Make Smaller Ecological Footprints!

An ecological "footprint" is the food, water and space that a living thing needs to grow and survive in an ecosystem.

Every thing that lives on Earth has a "footprint". Big things have larger footprints than little things. For example, a big tree needs more things to survive than a small flower!

Humans have ecological footprints too. Sometimes humans have very big ecological footprints. We use more things than we actually need. If we could make our ecological footprints smaller, then there would be more in our world to share with each other.

How can we make smaller footprints? Your job is to find out how!

You are now the teacher. Once you have completed this activity, you will visit another classroom in your school. You will present your bulletin board. Your board will teach others how humans can make smaller footprints. It will teach others how we can stop overusing our own environment.

USE THE FOLLOWING MATERIALS to put together a bulletin board:

- Bristol board
- Magazine pictures
- Scissors, glue, markers
- Any other materials you can think of!

Here are a few ideas to get you started.

To make smaller footprints, humans could ...

- recycle paper and containers
- ride a bike rather than driving a car
- take a shower instead of a bath to save water
- pick up litter
- turn the lights off to save energy
- Any more ideas?

 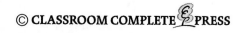

NAME: _____

Crossword Puzzle!

Across

1. group of things that live and work together in an environment
4. something that is not living
5. a microorganism that only has one cell
7. to use something again
8. used to look at something that is too small to see with eyes
10. when water turns from a vapor into a liquid
13. an organism that needs to be magnified to be seen

Down

1. food gives us this so that we can live a healthy life
2. tastes sweet and plants use it to make food
3. when water turns into vapor or steam
5. something that is living
6. an organism that depends on others for food
8. the path of water going around and around on Earth
9. when you gather something in one place
11. group of similar individuals living in the same area
12. organism that breaks down materials in dead organisms
14. something contagious that makes you feel unwell
15. a diagram that shows many food chains

Word List: abiotic, bacteria, biotic, collection, condensation, consumer, decomposer, ecosystem, energy, evaporation, food web, microorganism, microscope, population, recycle, sugar, virus, water cycle

Word Search

Find all of the words in the Word Search. Words are written horizontally, vertically, or diagonally, and some are even be backwards.

abiotic	decomposer	leaf	producer
bacteria	ecosystem	microorganism	recycle
balance	energy	nutrients	reproduce
biotic	environment	organism	succession
composition	evaporation	oxygen	sun
condensation	foodchain	photosynthesis	virus
consumer	fungi	population	web

b	a	c	t	e	r	i	a	v	e	e	c	n	a	l	a	b	n
w	o	d	r	e	c	y	c	l	e	r	t	h	t	n	v	b	u
e	e	r	c	o	n	d	e	n	s	a	t	i	o	n	z	c	s
n	t	z	g	w	e	f	g	t	y	x	b	q	e	r	z	o	t
v	n	c	w	a	r	n	u	t	r	i	e	n	t	s	q	n	s
i	o	v	s	q	n	w	e	c	o	s	y	s	t	e	m	s	h
r	i	b	d	w	e	i	j	w	w	r	w	j	h	s	a	u	e
o	t	b	f	y	n	f	s	r	e	d	b	k	g	d	p	m	e
n	a	n	g	u	b	g	h	m	d	c	v	f	f	e	h	e	h
m	r	y	g	r	e	n	e	t	w	w	a	b	d	c	o	r	e
e	o	g	h	g	v	h	r	y	k	e	r	g	s	o	t	n	e
n	p	h	r	n	o	i	t	a	l	u	p	o	p	m	o	l	y
t	a	p	j	e	c	y	b	y	n	g	d	x	w	p	s	r	k
v	v	j	r	h	p	j	v	c	g	d	h	y	e	o	y	y	s
r	e	k	k	o	q	r	c	u	i	n	m	g	r	s	n	e	u
e	t	y	v	j	d	u	o	o	w	t	b	e	t	e	t	d	c
b	b	i	k	t	u	x	d	d	s	o	n	y	r	h	s	c
n	i	g	r	b	r	k	c	e	u	w	h	i	h	m	e	c	e
m	o	n	u	e	e	r	w	e	d	c	a	v	b	n	s	n	s
r	t	u	s	w	q	w	e	r	r	y	e	d	f	a	i	v	s
y	i	f	o	o	d	c	h	a	i	n	h	g	j	k	s	v	i
k	c	c	c	o	m	p	o	s	i	t	i	o	n	r	y	e	o
g	q	e	m	s	i	n	a	g	r	o	o	r	c	i	m	s	n

After You Read

Comprehension Quiz

 30

Part A

Circle T if the statement is TRUE or F if it is FALSE.

8

T F **1.)** A rainforest, a puddle, our Earth, and a handful of soil are all examples of ecosystems.

T F **2.)** As long as organisms look similar, they are part of the same population.

T F **3.)** Succession describes what happens when something changes over a long period of time.

T F **4.)** Producers, consumers, and decomposers depend on each other for energy and food.

T F **5.)** Food chain shows how organisms rely on themselves to find food and energy.

T F **6.)** Photosynthesis is the process where plants use sunlight, water, and carbon dioxide to make food, oxygen, and water.

T F **7.)** The water cycle shows how water goes up through the roots of a tree, and falls back to the ground through evaporation.

T F **8.)** Microorganisms include big organisms like bacteria. They are so big that you need a telescope to see them.

Part B

Label the diagram by doing the following:

6

1. Write the stages below on the diagram to show each stage in the **water cycle**.

- evaporation
- condensation
- precipitation
- collection

2. Use a colored pencil to show the **path of the water** running through the water cycle.

3. What **shape** does your path make?

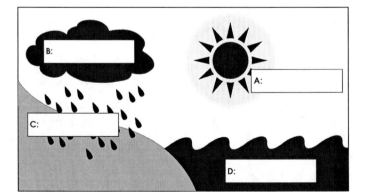

_____

SUBTOTAL: **/14**

Ecosystems CC4500

Comprehension Quiz

Part C

1. Describe what an **ecosystem** is. Give two examples of ecosystems and list what you might find living in each ecosystem.

4

_____

_____

_____

2. What two things are important to remember when describing a **population**? Give an example to show you understand the meaning of a population.

3

_____

_____

_____

3. Do **ecosystems change** over time? Describe **how** an ecosystem might change.

3

_____

_____

4. What is the difference between a **producer**, a **consumer** and a **decomposer**?

3

_____

_____

_____

5. Explain how **microorganisms** might be **helpful** <u>and</u> **harmful** to humans.

3

_____

_____

_____

SUBTOTAL: **/16**

3. Organisms reproduce with each other

4. Yes; If organisms don't reproduce, a population will not survive

5. Answers will vary

6. Answers will vary

(15)

**Answers will vary

(13)

1.
a) Ⓐ B
b) Ⓑ C
c) Ⓒ D
d) Ⓐ B

2.
a) Ⓕ
b) Ⓕ
c) Ⓣ
d) Ⓕ
e) Ⓕ

(14)

1.
1 — D
2 — B
3 — A
4 — E
5 — C

2. Answers will vary (i.e. communication between two or more people)

3. Answers will vary

(11)

Answers will vary

(12)

---

3. Answers will vary

4. Not all the same size

5. Answers will vary

6. Answers will vary

(10)

1.
1 — C
2 — D
3 — E
4 — B
5 — A

2.
a) Ⓕ
b) Ⓣ
c) Ⓣ
d) Ⓕ
e) Ⓕ

(9)

1.
a) ecosystem
b) biotic
c) balance
d) system
e) abiotic
f) environment

2. Answers will vary

3. Answers will vary

(7)

Answers will vary

(8)

4. Breaks down materials in dead organisms

5. They all depend on each other for food and energy

6. Answers will vary

1.
producer – **E**
decomposer – **C**
consumer – **D**
recycle – **A**
the sun – **B**

2. Into 3 categories: producers, consumers, decomposers

3. Producers make their own food, consumers depend on others for food

1. Answers will vary

2.
a) sun
b) decomposer
c) recycle
d) producer
e) consumer

Answers will vary

3. All parts of an ecosystem

4. Population may grow, shrink, or disappear; species might move into ecosystem

5. Answers will vary (i.e. cut down trees, develop land for houses)

6. Answers will vary

1.
a) every
b) ecosystems
c) composition
d) change
e) humans

2.
a) **F**
b) **T**
c) **F**
d) **T**
e) **T**

1.
a) Answers will vary
b) Answers will vary

2.
a) succession
b) ecosystem
c) biotic
d) environment
e) composition
f) population

Answers will vary

3. water, carbon dioxide, sunlight

4. plants, sunlight, energy, water

5. tree, cactus, fern plant

6. Answers will vary

7. Answers will vary

(33)

1.
a) ◯ B
b) ◯ D
c) ◯ A
d) ◯ D

2.
a) T
b) F
c) F

(32)

1.
a) photosynthesis
b) energy
c) leaves
d) carbon dioxide
e) sugar
f) oxygen

2.
PLANT: cactus, small tree, rose bush

ANIMAL: monkey, human, snake, puppy

3. Answers will vary

(30)

Answers will vary

(31)

3. Answers will vary

4. Answers will vary

(28)

1.
a) F
b) T
c) T
d) F
e) F

2.
1 — B
2 — E
3 — C
4 — D
5 — A

(27)

1. Answers will vary; links hold it together; the chain would fall apart

2.
a) web
b) interaction
c) nutrients
d) organism
e) chain

(25)

Answers will vary

(26)

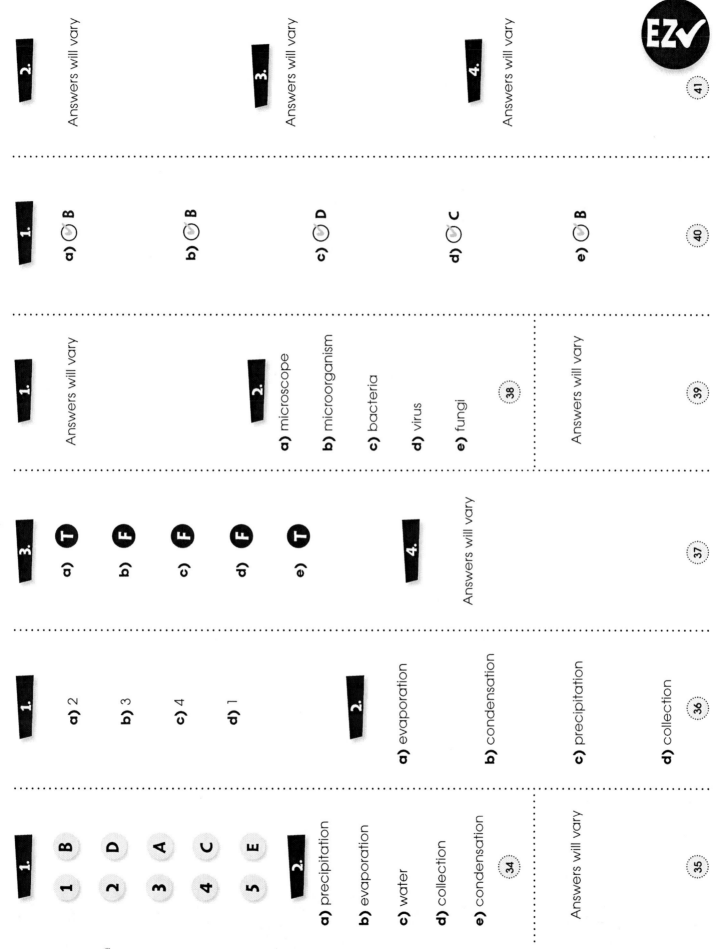

2. Answers will vary

3. Answers will vary

4. Answers will vary

1.
a) ◯ B
b) ◯ B
c) ◯ D
d) ◯ C
e) ◯ B

1. Answers will vary

2.
a) microscope
b) microorganism
c) bacteria
d) virus
e) fungi

Answers will vary

3.
a) **T**
b) **F**
c) **F**
d) **F**
e) **T**

4. Answers will vary

1.
a) 2
b) 3
c) 4
d) 1

2.
a) evaporation
b) condensation
c) precipitation
d) collection

1.
B 1
D 2
A 3
C 4
E 5

2.
a) precipitation
b) evaporation
c) water
d) collection
e) condensation

Answers will vary

34 35 36 37 38 39 40 41

Word Search Answers

Across:

1. ecosystem

4. abiotic

5. bacteria

7. recycle

8. microscope

10. condensation

13. microorganism

Down:

1. energy

2. sugar

3. evaporation

5. biotic

6. consumer

8. water cycle

9. collection

11. population

12. decomposer

14. virus

15. food web

Part A

1. **T**

2. **F**

3. **T**

4. **T**

5. **F**

6. **T**

7. **F**

8. **F**

Part B

1.

A: evaporation

B: condensation

C: precipitation

D: collection

2.

b) Pencil path should be a circle

Part C

1. Group of organisms that live and inter-act with each other; Examples will vary

2. 1) organisms are similar

2) live in same geographic area; Examples will vary

3. Yes, ecosystems change; Populations grow, shrink or disappear, species might move in.

4. Producers able to produce own food, consumers depend on others for food, decomposers break down dead matter to recycle

5. Helpful: medicine, food

Harmful: bacteria spreading, viruses

An Ecosystem

● ● ● ● ● ● ● ● ● ● ● ● ● ● ● ●

Producers, Consumers & Decomposers

Sun

Consumer

Producer

Decomposer

Soil

Sun

Producer

Consumer

Soil

Decomposer